Hello!
I am a rabbit.

I0108768

Rabbits have 360-degree vision.

I see you.

That means they can see behind them without turning their heads.

My whiskers are super sensitive.

A rabbit's whiskers help them feel around and find their way in small spaces.

Rabbits have a total of 24 whiskers.

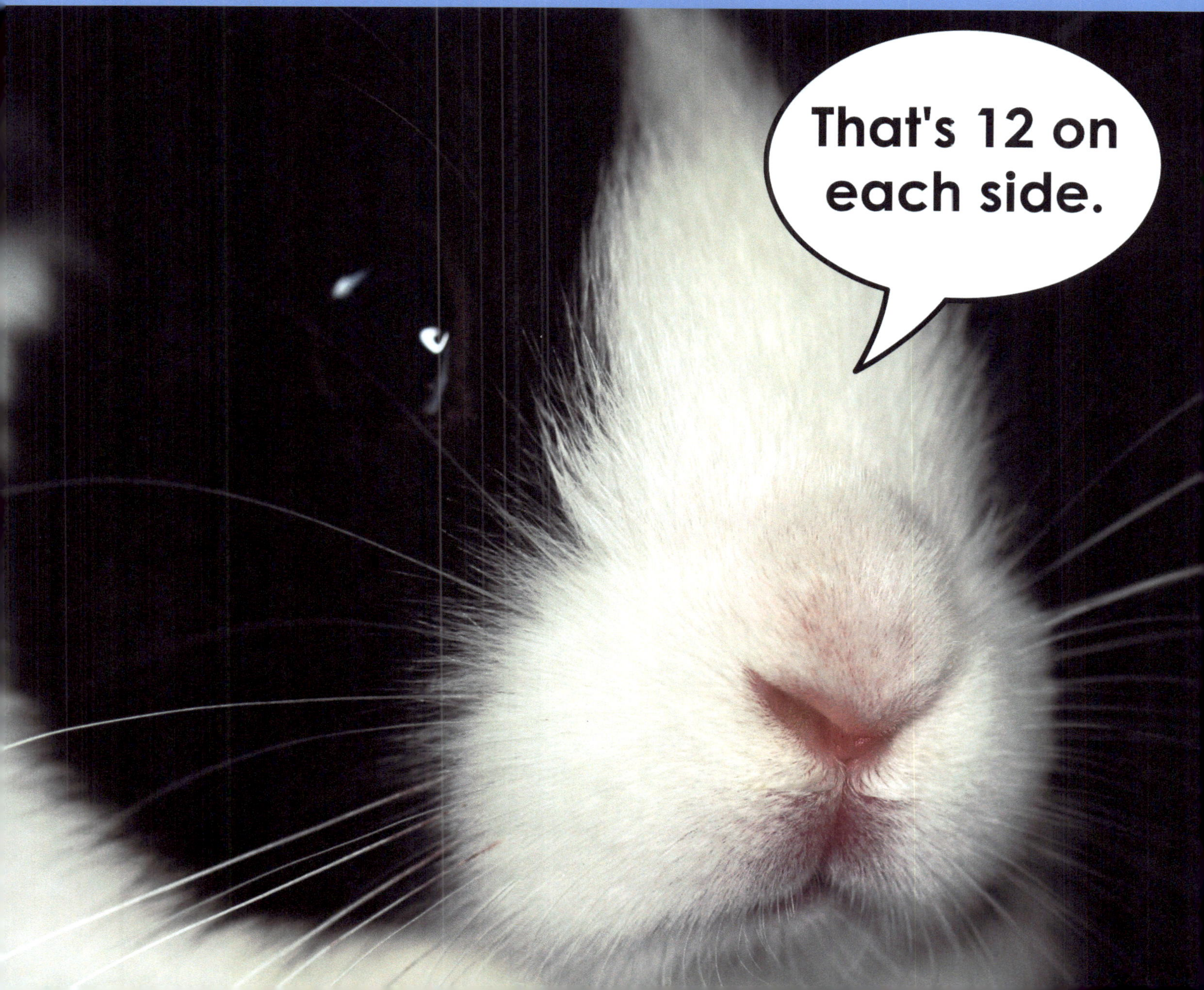

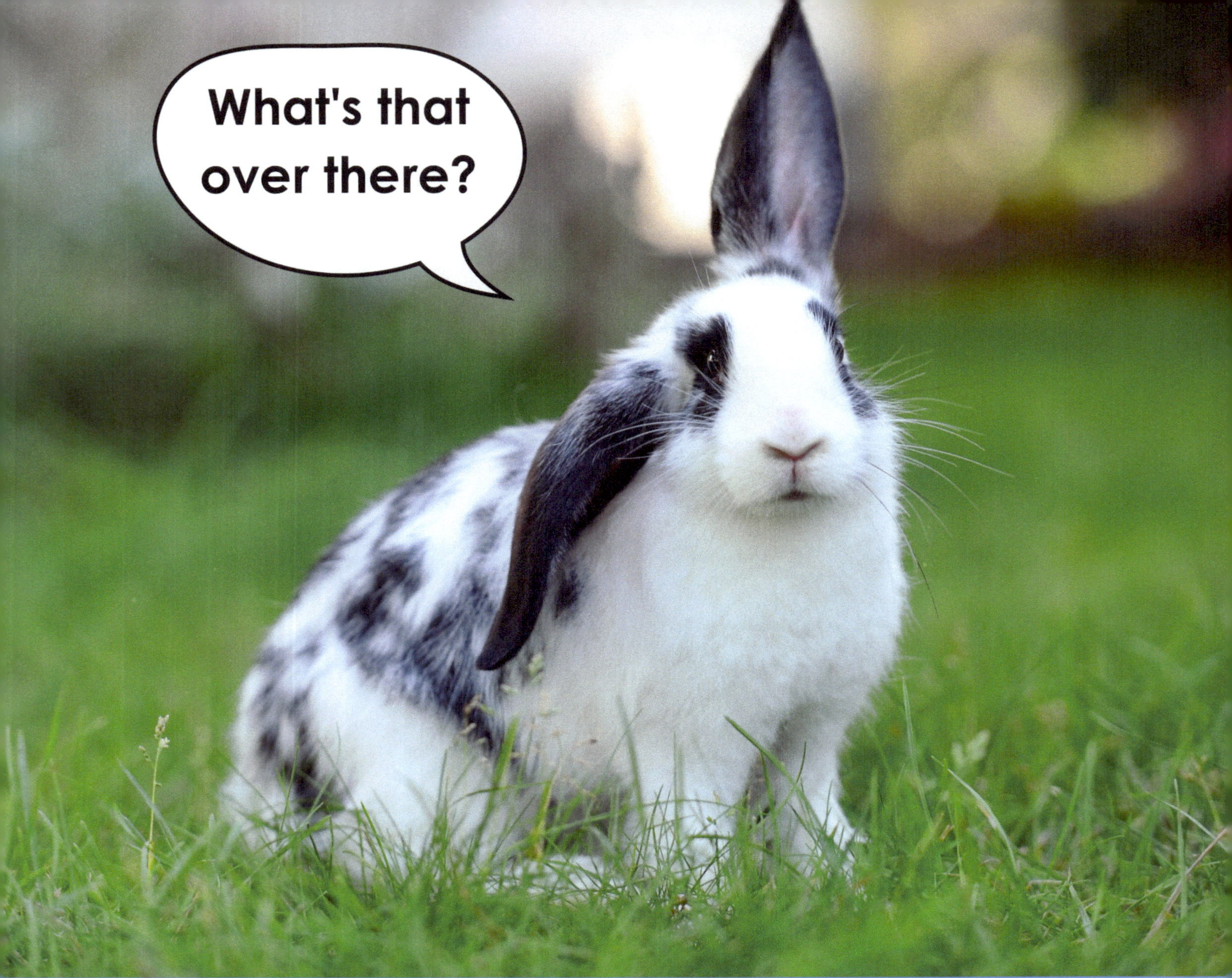

A rabbit can move each ear on its own.

When I'm happy or excited, my ears become warm.
When I'm scared, they get cold.

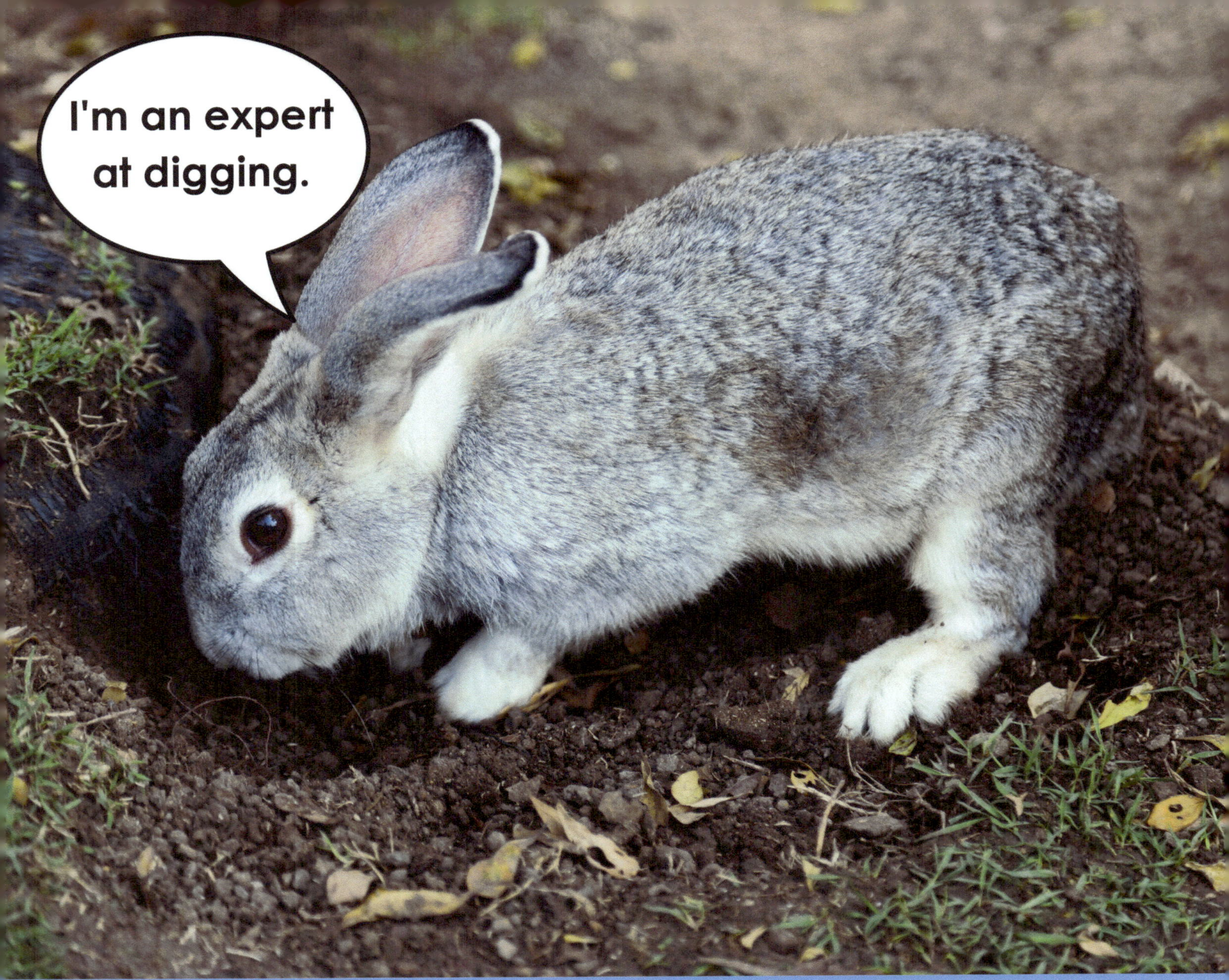

Rabbits dig underground tunnels called "warrens".

A warren can have multiple entrances.

My warren keeps me safe from predators.

Rabbits have powerful hind legs.

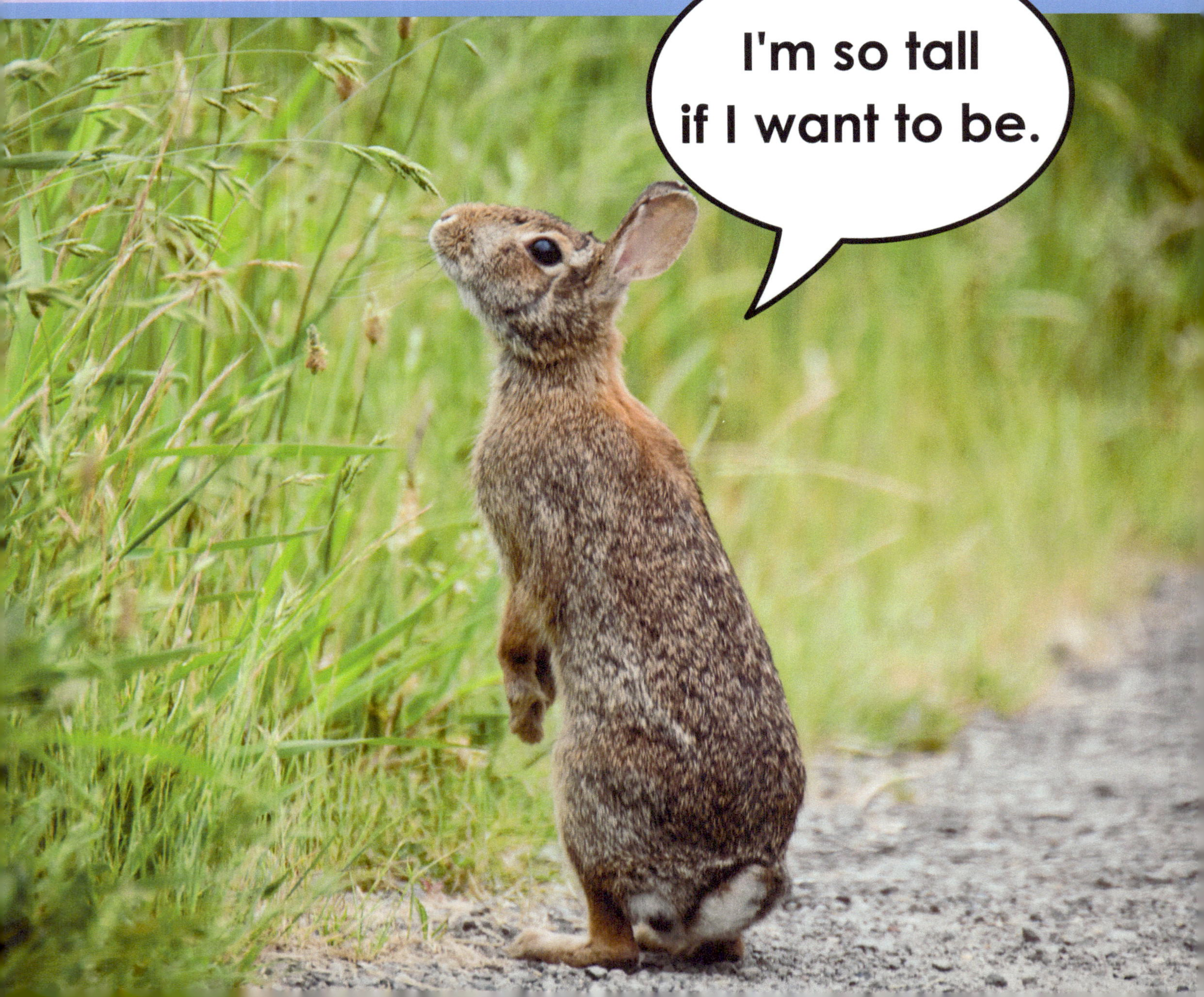

Rabbits can deliver powerful kicks with their hind legs to defend themselves.

Rabbits are excellent at hopping.

They can jump up to 9 feet (1m) across.

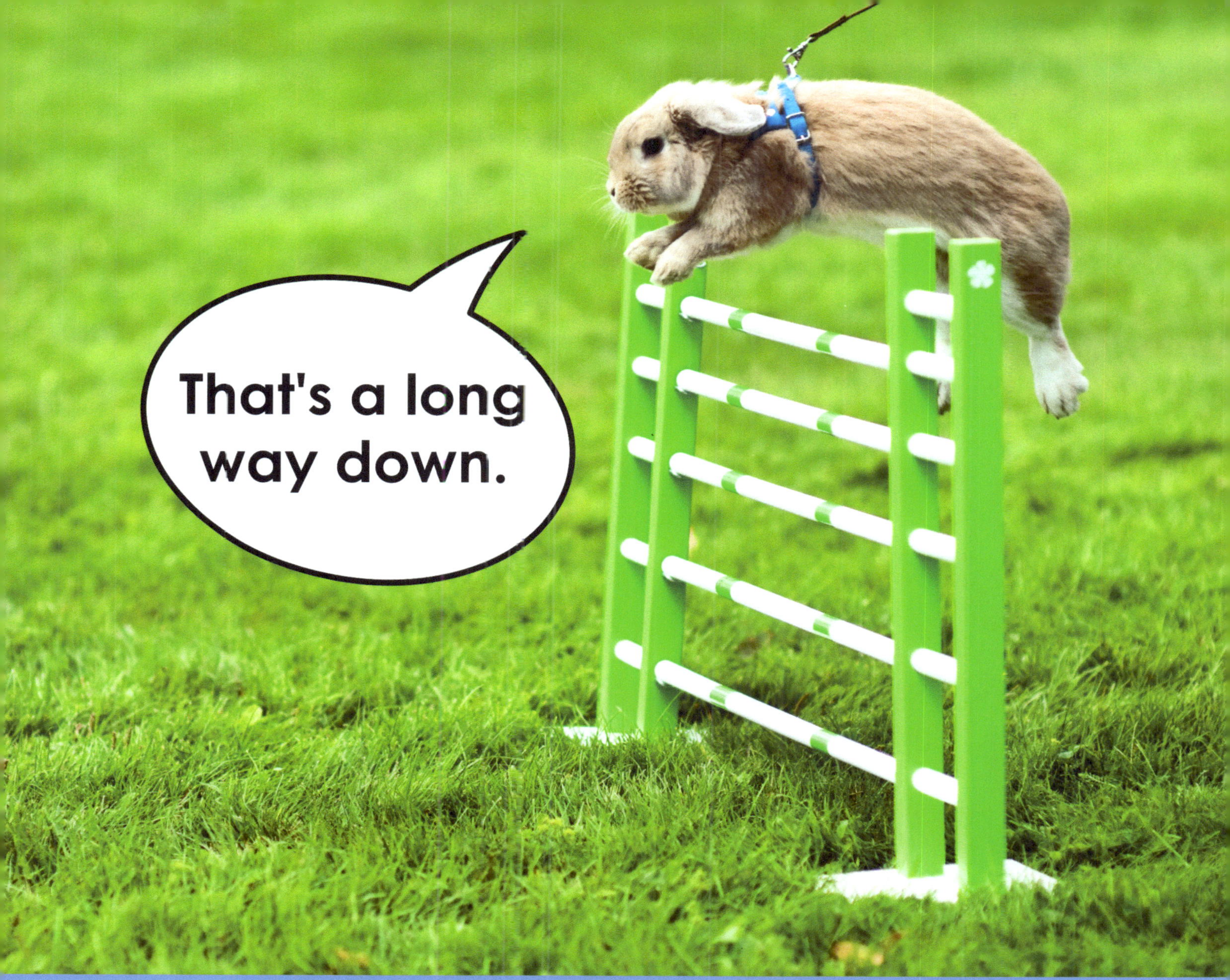
That's a long way down.

And they can jump up to 3 feet (1m) high.

A rabbit's front pair of long teeth never stop growing.

They need to keep biting hard objects or food to keep them short.

Does anyone have a carrot?

Rabbits are herbivores. They eat plants, grass, and vegetables.

Delicious and healthy!

Rabbits spend a lot of time grooming themselves.

Got to keep clean.

Looking good.

They lick their fur just like cats do to keep it clean and tidy.

Rabbits make different sounds like purring, growling, and even screaming to express their feelings.

Grrrrr...

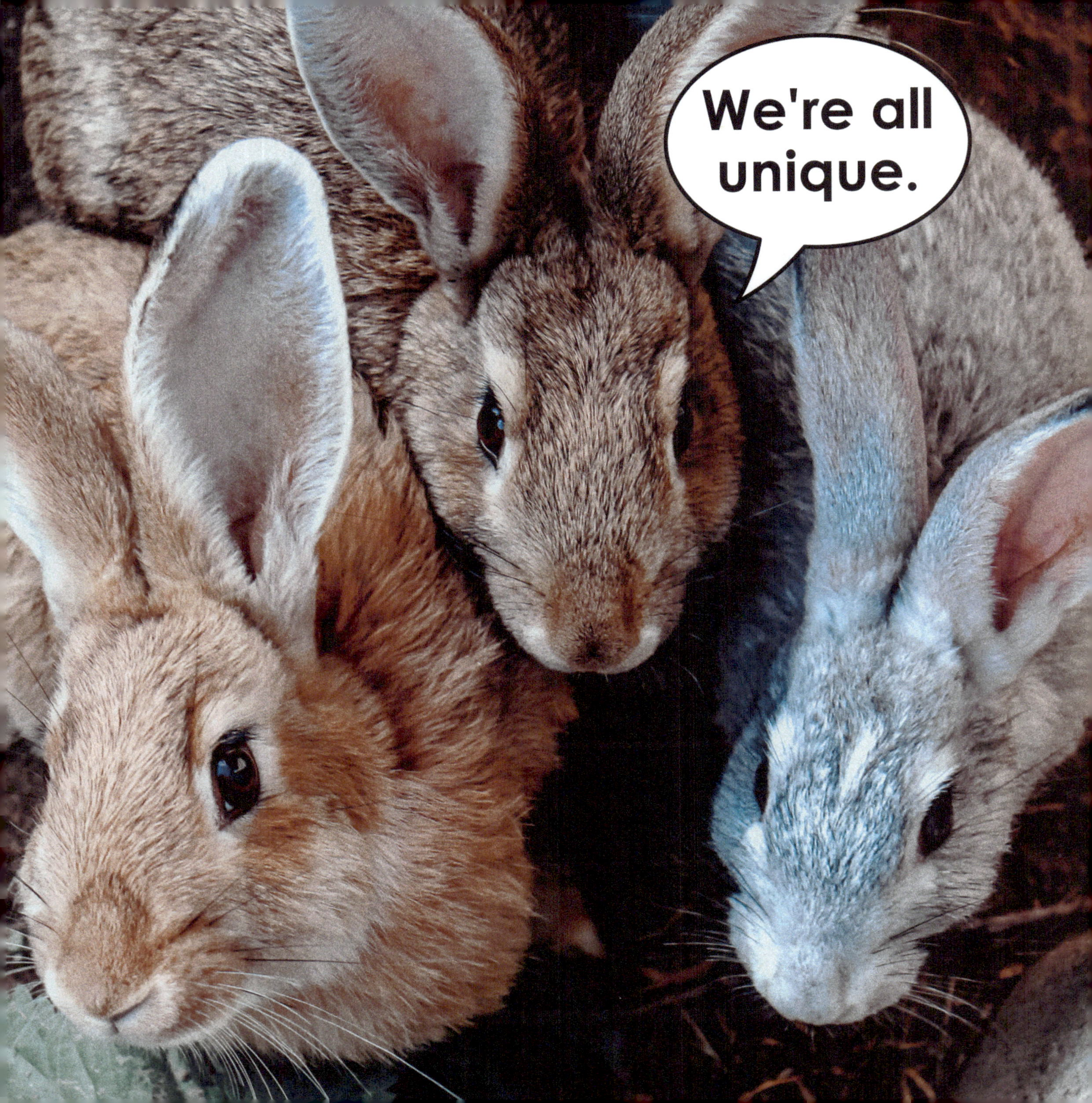
We're all unique.

There are more than 50 different breeds of domestic rabbits.

A group of rabbits is called a colony, herd, or warren.

Happy together.

A small colony has just
a few rabbits.

I think we're a big one.

A big colony can have
dozens.

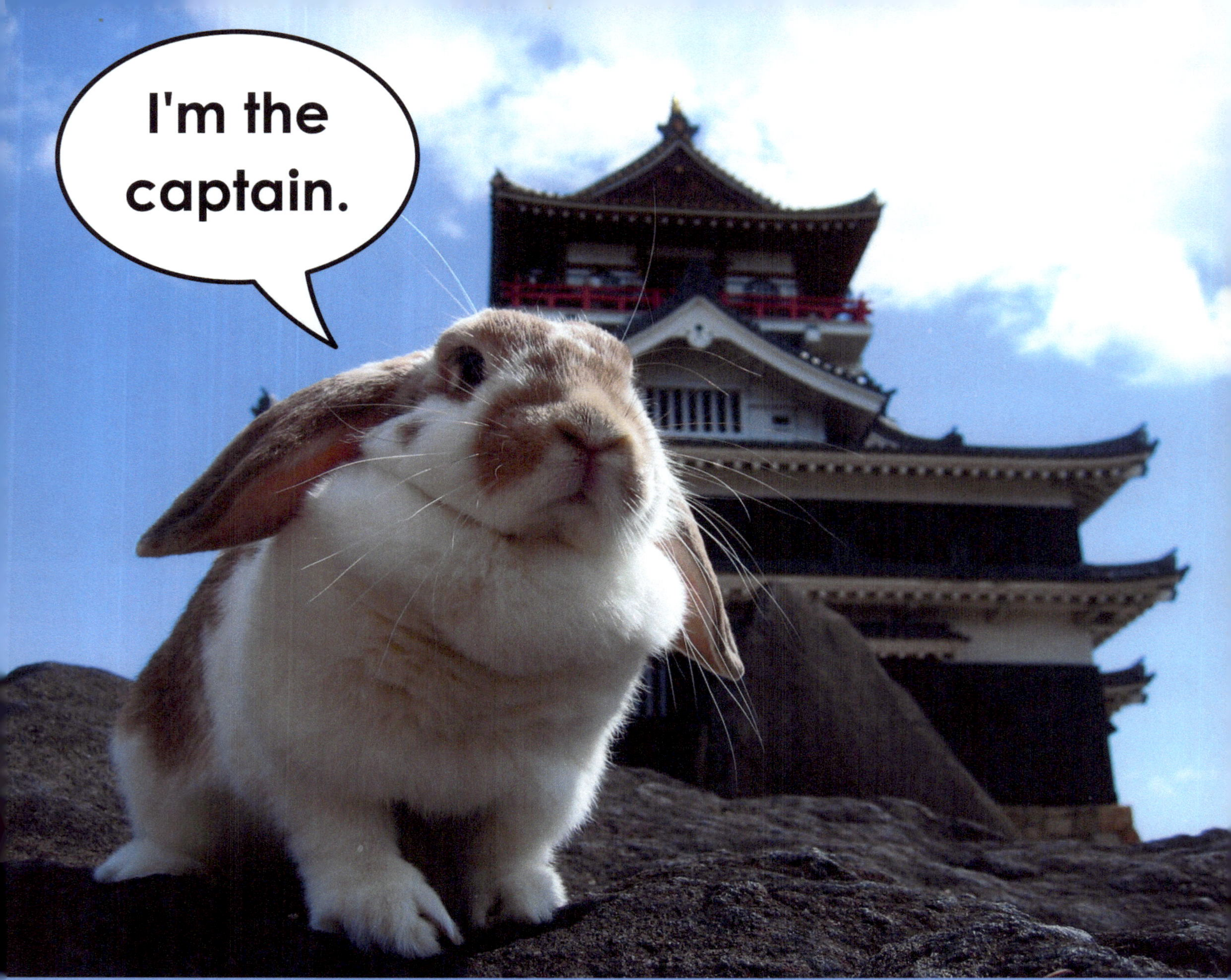

In each rabbit group, there is usually a leader rabbit.

The leaders get to choose their food and spots to rest.

Mother rabbits can become pregnant again just hours after they have a baby.

Baby rabbits are called kits or kittens.

When kits are born they are blind.

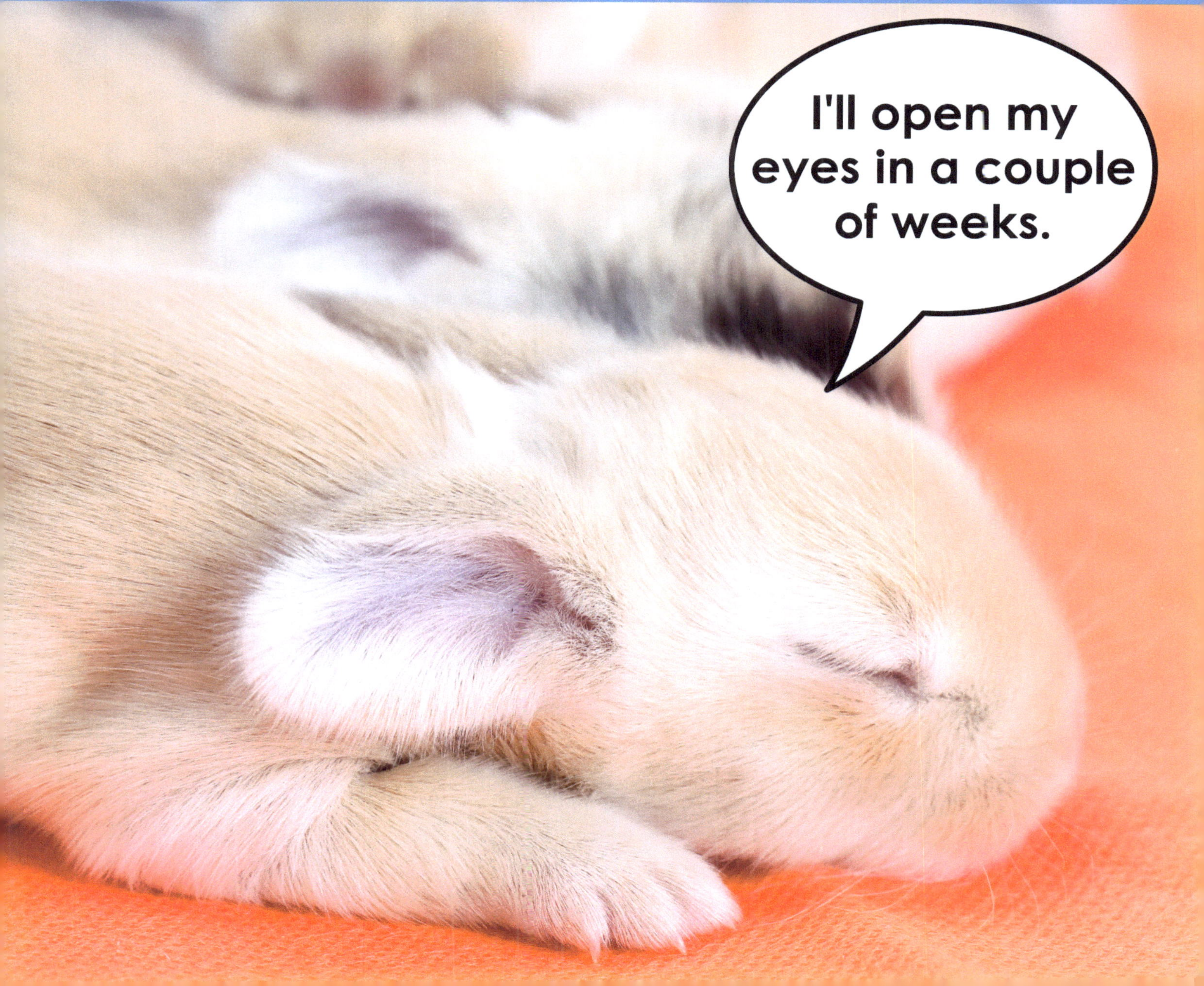

Rabbits have a powerful nose and a fantastic sense of smell.

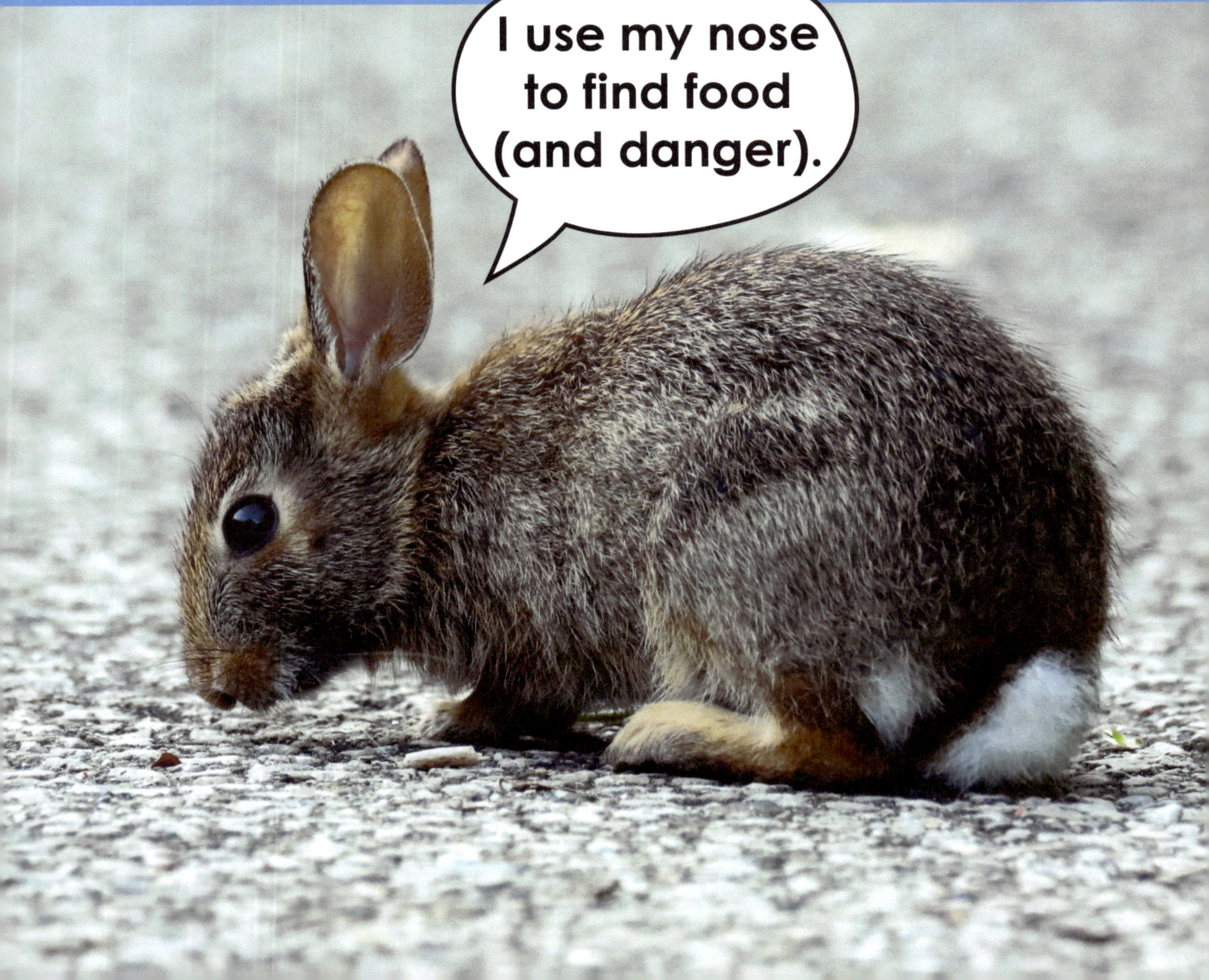

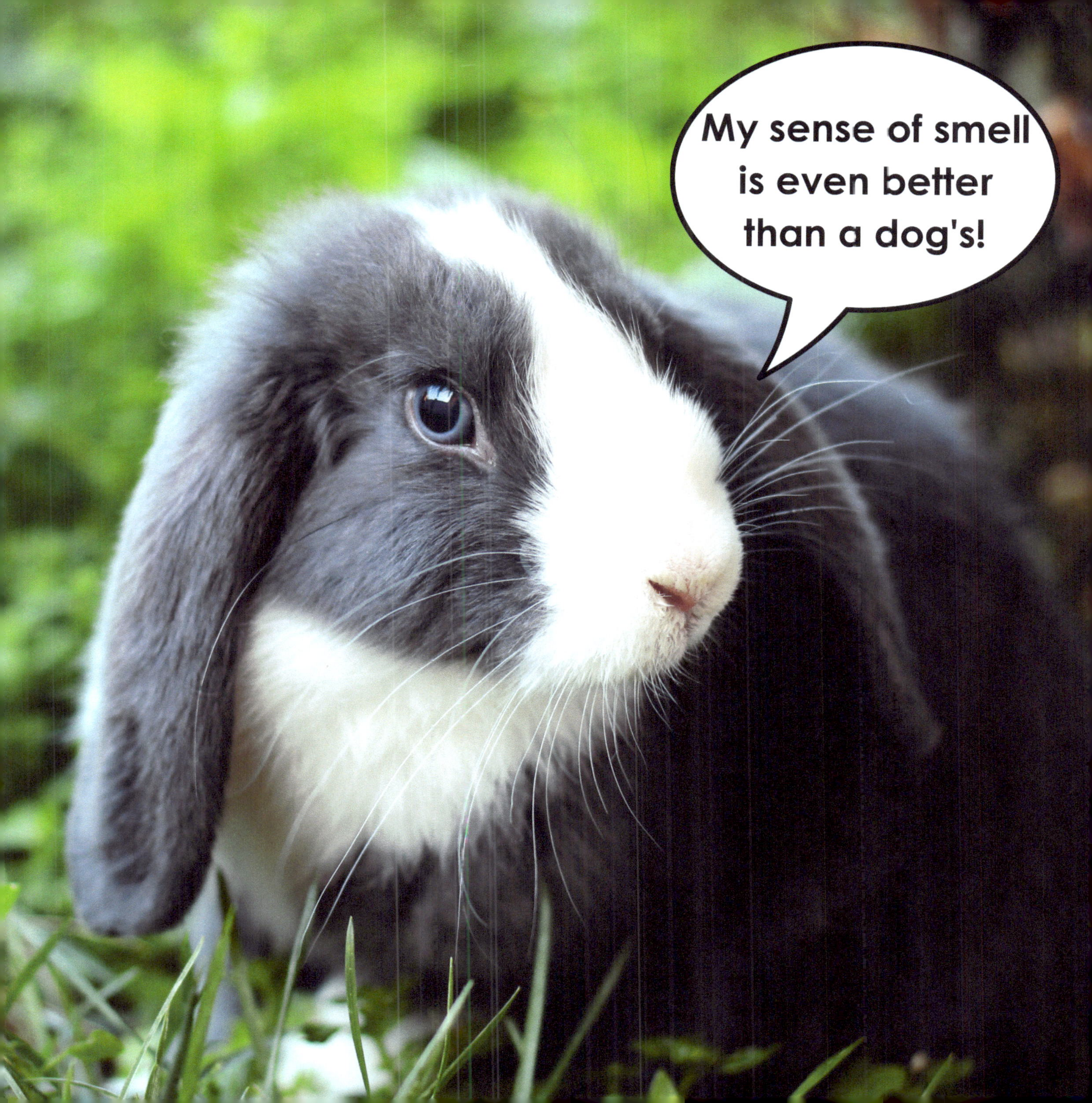
My sense of smell is even better than a dog's!

Want more?

... and more

Hello parents!

scan here

Visit us to find out about new releases and *FREE* offers. We'll let you know when we have a new release coming out and how you can get it for FREE.
And you can cast your vote for what book we make next!

ActiveBrainsBooks.com

or visit here

---◆---

scan here

Let us know what you think. As an independent publisher, your honest reviews mean a lot to us and our business. We'd love to hear from you!

amazon.com/review/create-review/

or visit here

---◆---

FOLLOW US on Amazon.

amazon.com/author/activebrainsbooks

ACTIVE BRAINS

ActiveBrainsBooks.com

www.ingramcontent.com/pod-product-compliance
Lightning Source LLC
Chambersburg PA
CBHW042056040426
42447CB00003B/245